Encore Love

Michael McCain

~Encore Love~

This book is a work of poetry. Unless otherwise noted, the author and the publisher make no explicit guarantees as to the accuracy of the information contained in this book and in some cases; names of people places have been altered to protect their privacy.

First Published for:
Maximize Publishing Inc. & Michael McCain

ISBN-13:
978-0615831176 (Maximize Publishing Inc.)

ISBN-10:
0615831176

Encore Love

Michael McCain

~Encore Love~

Table of Contents:

~Encore Love~

Dedication:

 I want to dedicate this book to love. I want to dedicate this book to every person who has suffered brokenness, depression and heartbreak. I want you to know love is still possible and your heart will heal.

I want to dedicate this book to my family, important love ones, and encouragers in the persons of:

Kelby Lott, Tongila Lott, Tabitha Dailey, Dasmine Dailey, Latavia Bew, Whitney Smith, Ashley Cain, Justin Maywhether, Astin Saddler, Kevin Brown, Kevin Neal, April Rivera, Kataisch James, Jolica Dale, Steven Dennis and Marvin Mixon.

~Encore Love~

Why I Wrote This Book

When I first felt led to put my heart on paper I had no specific title for what I would call this collection. I was in a place where my heart had been wounded so many times that it felt nearly impossible to love again. Not only was it time for me to grow past my past experiences but it was time to heal, forgive and learn to love again.

The title "Encore Love" came about as a whisper from God that I kept hearing in my spirit. I knew when I heard it that I would one day soon find love again. Yet while I observed my present life I had no present relationship or person to share my love with. What Encore Love means to me is that I have finally gained the victory and prevailed in life by finding someone that I love unconditionally and likewise loves me the same.

Encore Love simply means a repetition of a previous act; meaning that Encore Love means the power to love again; to repeat the act of loving as if the scars of your past did not exist.

~Encore Love~

If you are in have ever experienced hurt, bruising of your heart and feeling like you will never love and trust again, Encore love will revive your hope and cause you to fall in love again. Take this journey with me!

Part I

~Encore Love~

Fear of Love

Since the day I met you I knew I was in for it. It was like a head on collision and a deer struck by the glare of lights. I took one look at you and something shook the very core of my soul. Like a curious cat on the prowl I decided to chance my luck and see where fate would take me, as a matter of fact, where it would take us!

First it was the sound of your voice that warmed my heart and gave me heart flutters; the hours of conversation getting to know you and then came the vivid dreams of romantic evenings and intimacy with you. Dreams so real I could touch you, feel you, smell you, and taste you.

My mind often racing about what would love be like with you? What would life be like in your arms? Fear rises and reminds me I've tried this before but there's an angle of hope buzzing in my ear letting me know things will be much different with you.

I pray to dismiss all panic and my heart starts to melt for you. I'm losing this thing called fear of love.

What Does My Heart Say?

When I hold you in my arms at night and you lay your head on my chest what does my heart say?

As I feel your heart beat and you feel mine, what does my heart say?

When you close your eyes and hold me tight you give me the sense that you feel secure. I feel your submission and you begin to let go.

There are nights I can barely sleep as tears roll from my eyes and flood my ears. I no longer hear the sounds of the night but I'm soaking in my tears. Please forgive me, I'm far from sad. My heart is just very grateful to experience a love like yours.

What does my heart say?

I'm eager to know more of how you feel. I'm listening for answers I really want to know "what's the deal". I rest assured that we learn to love each other more and more each day. My question to you this day is what does my heart say?

No Longer Fallen

Here I go again opening the Pandora's Box. Feelings and emotions bubbling over for you I can't seem to control. I'm numb and I feel like I'm in a daze. I'm nervous when it comes to you. I used to think I was falling in love with you but I'm learning that it's far deeper than I expected.

Your eyes tell stories. I see a place much deeper that the surface. Your eyes tell the truth, it tells me you have been loved, hurt, broken and finding your place again. Your eyes give me strength and make me believe we can do this again we can do this thing called "love" again.

No longer fallen, I'm in love with you. I'm drunk with passion for you. I thirst for you like my necessary sustenance. I think of you often. I dream of you daily my heart beat for you.

I'm loving you...

I love you...

Every part of you; I accept you, flaws and all. I tremble when you touch me. My body quakes when you walk pass me. What is this I feel inside?

I'm loving you

Thinking of you always and forsaking all others. Embracing changes and making moves for progression.

I'm loving you

Past your past, in your present and into your future; I am covering you and showering you with prayers and love.

I love you.

No longer fallen!

Love You Forever

My heart feels full, it's one of the most content feelings I've ever had in my life. Every time I lay eyes on you I feel a fire burning inside me. You give me desires that I have not visited in a while. Your eyes take me on journey's they make me fantasize about our future and where we could be.

I want to love you forever...

Dismissing all fears and living in the moment. As long as I have you I feel like I have everything I've ever needed or wanted.

I want to love you forever...

Holding you tight, feeling your heart beat against mine, the warmth of your body gives me chills from head to toe.

I want to love you forever...

Give you the type of life fairytales are written about. You make me want to explore how many dreams can be a reality in one lifetime.

I want to love you forever...

Seal the deal and change your name. I'm thinking about our future kids and all. The dream life and home my heart tells me you derive.

I want to love you forever...

We have a passion so strong, a bliss that never seems to end. Your touch is erotic; your lips taste so sweet. Your skin's as soft as clouds.

I want to love you forever...

Sometimes I can't help but think about what took me so long to find you. Even in this moment I think about where I would be without you.

I want to love you forever...

Investing into you the best of everything I have to give, my love, my time, my body, my energy. My passion is overflowing for you, my heart burning for you.

I want to love you forever...

Encore Love

It was not so long ago I suffered a broken heart. I felt like I lost more in a day then some people have over years. Everything I ever held dear to me that once had value was now plummeted and trampled like a rush stampede in an evacuation emergency. Everyone close to me took something dear. Yet the one I love most at the time did the greatest damage. Out of the door went my love, my hope, my trust, my emotions, my dreams. Feeling broken abandoned and in need of refreshing.

Then there's the day I found you. I knew at first sight I would never be the same my inner instinct was confirming to me over and over again my change had come. We talked for days, yet when I laid eyes on you I felt liberated. Emotions began to open up again and I was left questioning my every action. Could it be possible that I am ready? Could it be possible that you're the one? Could it be possible we have something stronger than most?

Encore love...

Just when I thought I had given my best and I'm all washed-out. No energy left to invest in another relationship so I threw in the towel.

Encore love...

Just when my heart felt like it could not take another minute or last another day under the anguish of my loses I roll up my sleeves and put in the work; pulling myself up out of deep pit.

Encore love...

It's the part of you that's scared to love again but when you know you have found it that fear begins to dissipate. I'm letting go, you've found your way in.

Encore love...

Releasing all my reasons and excuses as to why I never wanted to try to love again. Excavating old memories and their demons; embracing today with new hope, faith and most of all love.

Encore love...

Just when you thought everything was dead you start to feel life again. I find myself saying encore...

Encore...

Encore...

I refuse to lie to myself I want more of you. I'm drunk at the very thought of you. I stagger; I'm in a daze daydreaming about the road and days ahead. As long as they are with you I'll be well. I salute you and take my bow, encore love!

Speechless

I am trying to find the words to describe how I feel about a love I found so true. You leave me in wonder and I find myself dumbfounded. I'm lost at words for trying to describe you. You wow me in ways that leave me in a constant state of bliss and amazement. Here I go again, speechless...

God give me the words to say, my heart feels overwhelmed, I've never been in this place before. I usually never miss a beat at expressing what's on my mind or what my heart has to say but you leave me exhaling and sighing with long pauses when I think about you. My heart is full you leave me speechless...

Who would have ever thought love like this was possible; who would have ever thought our paths would cross. I can honestly say I gave up on expecting love, finding love and when I gave up I found you. I am speechless because you embody everything I have ever wanted all my thoughts and dreams and silent prayers have been answered.

I am speechless.

If I could tell more of the truth there was a point in my life I knew not what to pray for. I can honestly tell you that I could have never prayed for someone more perfect than you.

I am speechless.

You give me reason for living; I feel I have something someone to fight for. I feel my strength coming back and new life springing up within me. I have the nerve to think about the future again when it was once so painful. I have new love, new faith, new hope, new joy and I am completely speechless.

My Biggest Secret

I have a secret and its killing me inside. I have a story and a history I want to let go of. I pray every day that it never hinders me from loving you. It causes me to cringe when I think of all the things that I have been robbed of because of this. I lost what I felt was the world, family, friends, money, connections and could not even see the most important thing I was left with was LIFE.

Can I tell you my secret? I am sure there are times when you look me in my eyes and you can see it. My eyes may not always be glossy with thankfulness sometimes the truth is its pain, its fear, its shame, its abandonment. Every time you hold me in your arms it heals me. It helps me to let go. It reminds me to live again. I can feel fresh life coming back into my being. I feel grateful for a love like yours. There's moments where demons invade my mind and tell me I don't deserve your love.

My biggest secret is loving you is teaching me how to let go of the past. I confess that I was not as strong as I thought I was, right before meeting you I nearly broke. You gave me your hand and now I feel new strength. When I hold you I get the sense that you needed me as much as I needed you.

My biggest secret is that fear sometimes grips me of losing you, of doing something foolish or something breaking us apart. I am learning that I have kept the past alive so long that it doesn't want to let me go. I am leaving to dismiss the STORY that I have been holding on to and embrace the future I am building with you.

I confess today, to love you forever. Live in the now and forget the past. Make every moment memorable and honor everything you do. I vow to love and cherish you, honor and keep you near. I vow to always give you the best that I have and never second best; most of all I vow to love you unconditionally and that my love is no secret.

Long Goodbye

I want you to listen to what my heart is saying to you today, sit still and hold your pace, I promise to make this real short. You're everything I've always wanted. You're more than I have ever dreamed of. You complete me in places I could not have imagined. You heal places I never knew were broken. They say all things have its end. I have decided to love you with everything I have. I vow till death do us part, let's make it a long goodbye. Let's love each other with everything we've got. I think our love has all the ingredients to show the world what real love is. It's unconditional, patient, kind, gentle, thoughtful, passionate, romantic, and sensual.

 One day our road will end but until then I want to hold you like every day was the last, kiss you like every time was the first time, make love to you as if we were virgins, hold your hand going down a long winding road, cuddle with you as if tomorrows never coming. I don't know what our future holds, how long you'll be here, how long God has given me this gift of loving you. I don't know how long this love will last, but do me a favor would you please? Let's make it a long goodbye.

Fever

Here I go again, another sleepless night you would think I would be cool by now lying next to the one I love so dearly. My heart is racing as you lay your head upon my chest I am vividly daydreaming about future moments with you and where I want to see us end up. Then I feel my manhood rise up I am so conflicted I know not whether to pray or follow my passion. The way you submit to me completely turns me on and I am lost at how to fulfill my desire. I am burning deep down within me to express everything I feel and what I feel is not completely sexual although I have to admit I am feeling a bit sensual thinking about past times and the love that we have made it just makes my body crave you the more. I wonder in my mind what does our future have in store. I am willing to give up, just let go and let it all happen. I feel like I have tried and tried to love so many times and I have come up empty. It would be completely unfair to you to withdraw from this relationship now. I am in way too deep and every part of me needs you and I am scared to death because I know it. You give me fever. I shake with night sweats thinking about how deeply I love you. I am shaken with fever when I think about how warm I feel inside when I hold you close.

Fever...

When the tears roll down my eyes there's nothing I am sad about just completely grateful that God would entrust me just one more time to have a love so true and I can't believe I am holding you. I completely gave up on finding love and everything about this relationship makes me fight. Makes me fight to live again, love again, want again, desire again to be deeply entangled and one again with someone you give me fever, I am shaking so deep within. I have had lust, I thought I knew love, but know that I hold you I know fear, the fear of finally finding what you desire most and now you're afraid you're not completely ready. I have to shake this fever and draw you nearer to me. Hold me tight while I drift away, I must silence my mind from thinking so much. You give me chills, you give me hope, and you give me fever.

Erotic Passion

I am laying here in your arms and I tend to drift away to a place full of so much bliss. I think about your sweet caramel lips and the way your hips wrap around my waist and then I loose myself. I think about the way your hands rub my chest and then I can feel the heat rise between me and you, sometimes I swear it's mostly me thinking so passionately about you. I try to calm myself, as I feel my manhood rise up and I feel completely sexual. I can feel my heart racing and I am trying to control emotions that seem to rush all over me.

I feel completely erotic.

Thinking about things we have not tried yet when we make love. In my heart and in my mind our love life is just as new as the day we started and it never grows old. As a matter of fact each day I fall completely and more madly in love with you.

I feel completely erotic.

It has to be a spell or maybe its lies you tell that you love me as deeply as I love you.

When I look in your eyes I know it can't be lies
that you tell because I feel love from a place
so deep I can't possibly describe I feel like a
weaving basket and we have been sown
together and there's just no separating.

I feel you.

I want you desperately but I already have you,
I want to completely express what I feel but
will you understand that it has nothing to do
with your body? Maybe this is a man thing and
I just don't know how to express what I feel
without being physical but everything about
you turns me on and you completely woo me. I
feel so much passion for you I need a release
please tell me you feel what I feel. I feel
drunken at times when I look in your eyes your
eyes take me places I know I have never been.
What is it that you do to me that makes me
feel this way? I am drunk with passion.

~Encore Love~

Part II

~Encore Love~

Crave

I crave your mouth, your voice your hair. I crave your touch the sweet smell of your skin. I crave your laugh in my ear and the way you hold me near. I crave you touch and the way you run your hands down my bicep's. I crave your sweat, the way we burn with passion and drench each other leaving each other laying with cold sweats. I crave the way you leave me breathless, speechless, and unable to find words to convey and express maturely and intelligently the way I feel about you inside out.

I crave you.

I crave more of the way your hips sway and the fragrance you leave behind I kiss you goodbye in the mornings. I crave the love I feel when you submit to me and lay you head on my chest at night. I feel so much peace when you're near me. I crave the way you put your heart and soul into when you cook, the way you look in my eyes and tell me that my existence makes you feel needed. I crave your smile when your frustrated and there's nothing to smile about I work overtime to pull the happiness up out of you.

 I crave you.

The rest of my life with you, I am ready to give my life for you. I am ready to fully commit to what we have together, you give me desires I thought I could never revisit. You open portals in my heart I promised never to revisit you have captured me and I feel over taken and I wonder sometimes why do I let you in but I feel so weak cause every part of me wants you and desires you and I know deep within me I need you. Look me in my eyes and tell me today that you love me that you want me as much as I want you because... I... Crave... You...

When I say I can't

If you know anything about me know there are times you can't listen to me because I say one thing and inwardly want another.

Like the times I tell you I can't go no further really means I want more of you.

Like the times I tell you I am completely confused really means I have made up my mind and I just can't believe I have changed my old mindsets.

Like the times I tell you just give me time, when I really mean were not moving fast enough.

Like the times I tell you I trust God, when I really mean if I have to work it out with my bear hands I will do it for you.

Like the times I tell you I am stressed out when in reality I am completely frustrated about making everything perfect for you.

Like the times I tell you I can't sleep when I am really up day dream and mind racing about my future with you.

 Like the times I tell you take my last, when I really mean that I'll be willing to give you everything I have left if it pleases you.

Like the times when you tell me to rub your body and I tell you I am not trying to be sexual but can't resist the passion I feel.

Like the times I tell you I want to go to bed early, when I really want you to just come and hold me, I feel so selfish I ball myself up in a knot.

Baby, there comes a time that if you know me and know me best, know there are times when I tell you I can't that you can't either, do the very opposite of whatever I say, those are the moments when I need you most; Because I can't do it without you.

Kiss

How many years I must have yearned
for someone's lips against mine. I am talking about
lips that are completely mine and no one else's.
How many nights I longed to get lost in some long
flowing hair they I found myself entangled in yours.
There's hardly any air we becoming one so deep.

Kiss me again, reaching that place
that sends messages to toes and fingertips,
Then all the way to something like home where the
heart is.
I then hear music was playing on its own and
there's not a soul or a song playing.

Nothing like a love who knows how and where
to kiss the right thing at the right time,
Then kisses the things on me you have missed.
How had I ever settled for less? How can I ever live
without the rest of what you have to offer? I just
can't part with you or those lips.

I was thinking this is intelligence,
this is the wisest tongue
 you're like a goddess in a Greek Gods ear,
Speaking sense. It's the Good, the bad, the lovely
and I understand it all the things you speak.

It's the kiss you leave me with that makes me weak, it makes my knees buckle and my heart skips beats and yes I am completely weak over you. You have power over me with those soft lips and you use them like a weapon, because you know I desire more and more of that kiss.

This Love

You are my love, my love, my heart; my soul is my gift to you.
Your smile, your love is the only reward I would want or ever need. You complete me each time we embrace. Your love takes me to a foreign place. I am no longer afraid and I am giving it all that it takes. You mean everything to me, so I give my all and put it all up for takes.

You're precious, like a gem made by the hands of God to shine forever.
When we make love I release the passion inside me that burns for you.
Each day just at the very thought of you I feel as if angels are intertwining our destinies, so

that we two soul mates will forever live in harmony.

Now and forever, I'll do all that it takes to live out our hopes and dreams.

Creating our own bond of life, to overcome the challenges that we will face, you give me strength and joy that I can trace back to good days and bad days , I love them all cause I spent them with you.

Let's take some time to explore the mysteries, and to enjoy life as it should be. Let's just make the love we have last, making it a long goodbye.

Sharing the peace and love, that everyone looks for. Let's celebrate the fact that we have everything we need in this love together. You complete me and I am complete with you, I am happy, healthy and whole.

So in the end I want nothing, because I have everything I need with this love!

What I Love About You

I love the way you look at me, it makes me completely weak and I give into you. You leave me breathless and speechless I am struck over and over again by you. I love your eyes so bright and deep brown.
I love the way you kiss me, your lips so soft and smooth. Every kiss is like a touch of heaven.

I love the way you make me so happy, there's joy inside me that I often can't explain but every day and every moment with you I get to live it over and over again.
I love the way you show me the ways you show you care.
I love the way you say, "I Love You,"
And the way you're always there.

I love the way you touch me, it sends a ripple effect of emotions not just through my body but my soul.
When you touch me I am left completely weak, it always sending chills down my spine.

I love that you are with me; out of the many men on this earth you could have chosen, I'm glad that you are mine. My heart just wanted to express in dearest form what I love, what a love, what I love about you.

When I First Looked Into Your Eyes

When first I looked into your eyes each breath became a thousand sighs. Since then I've been trying to understand what it is that you do that makes me weak and breathless. My heart drums out a beats like thunder bolts cracking the sky. Every day I glow with joy from head to toe. The hand of love has touched my soul; I feel wedding bells all down in my soul. Everything in me confirms a thousand times over that you have to be the one I wanted for, cried for, prayed for and longed for. I can feel myself drifting away like a boat at sea; the tide of love began to rise,
my world now filled with summer skies. My skies were once clouds of cold and grey. Then

you came along and brightened each day, that look in your eyes glowed with gold, and then whisked my heart away.
There are mornings I wake up to the sounds of birds singing me love songs while I hold you hear. Can you hear the birds singing our favorite song?

The air is filled with lovebird cries, when I first looked into your eyes. Something shook me down to the core and center of my soul I knew then I had to make you completely mines. Not one day would I ever want to spend alone without you I am holding you tight, I want us to be together keeping each other warm all through the night.

When I first looked into your eyes, something completely magical happened. It was as if all time and space were paralyzed. In that day and moment the worlds stopped just for us, I could barely catch my breath and in that instant, I was shown a universe I had never known. A new world and a new love I would be sharing with you. Made me question what world did I live in before I met you?

 Because I chose you and you choose me I now dwell there still, in Paradise, a love so complete and true, my own touch of heaven while yet on earth is what I feel when I look into your eyes.

Motionless

If time could stand still, I'd freeze it here, so you'd always hold me, close and near. In your arms, where I'm meant to be, there's no other place in this world I'd rather be. Filled with the perfect love you've given me. A love so perfect so kind so true, I get to live it every day that I am with you.

A bond so strong, a hold so tight, to know you're the one; my 'Mrs. Right'.
A blessing sent from up above, in you I've found my one true love. I can end my search and freeze all time here. I want to have this moment for life.

Our lives entwined to be as one, to have and to hold, a love story that will never grow old. If I could freeze time I'd stop right here to create a lasting memory of this love for eternity. I'll take my chances be as it may, to let time do its job and I'll do mine upon this journey we've just begun; where you and I together will find no less, than eternal love and happiness.

Perfect Love

I prayed for the perfect love to come my way, I was so blind with pain I nearly missed God's answer. I found a love without searching, I prayed and like a gift you appeared, present.

All I ever wanted was to be part of your heart, to have a love that loves and accepts me for who I am. When I found you it was definitely love at first sight. All I wanted was for us to be together, to never be apart.

No one else in the world can even compare, you're perfect and so is this love that we share. Your good to me, you're good for me, and I want you to know that every part of me needs you.

We have so much more than I ever thought we would,
I love you more than I ever thought I could. I

don't know where the strength comes from, but I find myself sacrificing miracles to be with you. I can admit I may not be perfect or have it all but you pull a better person out of me.

I promise to give you all I have to give; I'll do anything for you as long as I live. I'll fight for you; die for you if I have to. I realize we only have this one life to live, so let's live it to the fullest and love each other completely.

In your eyes I see our present, our future and past, each moment spent with you is easing the stains from our past. This is a love that heals me, this is the love needed for me. By the way you look at me I know we will last.

I hope that one day you'll come to realize, how perfect you are when seen through my eyes. If I were you I would just let time take its course, don't try to change a thing. Our love gets deeper and better with time. Do you see it like I see it? We have the perfect love.

A New Day

It's a new day, full of joy and moments to be spent with you.
I look into your love drunken eyes and I feel like a flower in full bloom. My cheeks instantly get rosy and my heart feels warm inside.
I feel the old things are passed away and now I am beholding a new beginning. With you at my side how can I go wrong?

You gave me new reasons to keep fighting, to keep living, to keep loving. You empower me to be a better man, greater lover and every moment with you feels blessed.

It's a new day.

I no longer have to dream about a love that's all mine.
No more looking over my shoulder and wondering if we will make it.
I am learning to let go.
I am learning to have faith.
I am learning to trust again.

It's a new day.

Each time you hold my hand, cress my face
with your soft and gentle skin I get new
strength. You thrill me and my heart is full with
bliss. I could not have prayed for a more
perfect love if I made it up as a fairy tale.

It's a new day.

I am embracing every moment with you
Loving a little harder, laughing a little longer,
and smiling from the inside out.
The love that we share heals me; it removes
all the pain and doubt. I lift my eyes toward
heaven and thank God for this new day!

Afterglow

It's the thought of you after you touch me.
It's the ripple effect I feel after you kiss me.
It's the residue of your sweet smelling skin
after your warm body has been pressed
against mine.

It's the whisper of your voice in my ear.
It's your gentle touch that casts away all fear.
It's the memories that we created that keeps
you're ever present.
It's your unconditional love that sparks my
ambition.

It's the joy you bring my when I see the smile on your face.

It's the hope that you give me that revives my heart.

It's the dream of our future ever bright, ever present and pressing near. How dare I give up now?

It's the afterglow.

The pep in my step

The smile on my face

The reason my heart beats

The reason my joy remains full

It's the afterglow.

Loving you is a powerful elixir

I am drunk with purpose

Were pregnant with destiny

We're provoking change in each other's life.

I am glowing.

I am glowing with you, for you and because of you.

Part III

~Encore Love~

Intense

When I think of you a rush takes over my mind, my body, my soul.

Sometimes I cry when I think of you, my heart is full of gratitude that God would afford me to love someone like you.

I am overwhelmed when you reciprocate the love that God gives me to give you.

It's intense.

When you give of yourself when you have nothing left

It's intense.

When you cry with me tears of joy and celebrate our ups, downs and victories.

It's intense

When I wake up in the morning and I see your face next to me. Reminding me I spent one more night with the love of my life.

It's intense.

When you come home to me, letting me know you survived the day's trials and temptations and I once again kiss your sweet lips.

Every day I grow more and more in love with a beautiful person and loving you is completely intense!

Why I Love You

I've grown a lot since I've been in love with you.

You give to me hope, you empower me to cope.

When life pulls me down, you smile your wisdom brings me around.

You teach me that is still possible to love and care. You help me to share.

~Encore Love~

You make me honest and shared the deepest sentiments of my heart.

From you I've learned love; with grace from above we endure and grow more and more in love.

It's for you that I love, I give, and I thrive to be a better person from day today.

You are the reason I have learned to love, to give, to be selfless. You have become that reason to put someone first, forsaking all others.

You are the reason that fills each season of my life.

When I hear the word love I think of you.

When I hear the word love I can feel you.

When I say the word love I taste your name.

Every time I think of love I think of you.

~Encore Love~

You are my world and my best friend.

I love your heart, because you are so kind, thoughtful and caring.

I love you because you are pleasant, honest and daring.

I could never imagine how someone could not love someone like you.

You made me the man I am today.

Today now and forever I LOVE YOU.

Thank you.

Deep

Have you ever loved something, someone more than you love yourself?

You find that the very essence of what makes you wake from day to day is the fact that you have someone to wake up to, someone to hold your hand. Have you ever felt that if your breath left your body you would lose your purpose?

I am talking about your reason for living.

I am talking about the love that you share that's deep, intimate and passionate.

The type of love that makes you day dream and leaves you with night sweats when you think about the memories and the passion you share.

Going deep

The type of love that exceeds any hurt or pain you have ever experienced. All your days of regret and dismay washed away.

Deep

Like the wounds that once ate at your heart like cancer and now you grip your chest not from the pain but from heart flutters.

Deep

How old memories can be erased while creating new ones with the one you love.

Deep

How far the tears run when I cry, it's full of thankfulness, gratefulness and wonder at how I deserve a love like yours.

Deep

When I hear the key turn in the door; my eyes water because you're coming home to me. When my past was full of horror stories and wonder of where my love could be.

Deep

When you put me first, shower me with love and share kisses of "Just because".

Now and forever I want to celebrate this love we share because it's a love that runs "Deep".

Pieces of a Dream

You're like pieces of a dream I once had; a fairytale that I would runaway to in my mind. Your kisses are like déjà vu, they take me to spiritual places that I have been with you.

Pieces of a dream

The fragrance you leave in the room that lingers that reminds me of our passion; nights of love making and laughter.

Pieces of a dream

The blossoming reality that everything we are currently sharing is as real as it gets. I have no regrets.

Pieces of a dream

Your smile makes me feel warm inside, some thoughts of you make me shake and I get chills down my spine.

Pieces of a dream

Spending sunrises and sunsets with you; going for walks and holding your hand tight. You make my palms sweat and I am not even the nervous type.

Pieces of a dream

Drunk with an elixir of love I see it all in your eyes, the way you look at me, you take my breath away.

Pieces of a dream

Sometimes all I can think about is you. My heart wants to please you, romance you and love you endlessly.

Pieces of a dream

You leave me with wonder, how did you ever make it into my life. I don't believe in luck, it just doesn't exist in my world. I now know from loving you just how blessed I am.

Life and love with you is nothing more than pieces of a dream.

Relax

I can see you have had a long day.

I see the spaced out and empty expression over your face.

I can see how flushed your supple skin looks and the twinkle that's fading from you eye.

I can see the extra sway in your hips that doesn't come from pep in your step but rather a drag in pulling yourself along the way.

I can feel the sign from across the room; even in the silence it speaks volumes.

I want to take the load off you, help you unwind and relax your mind.

Let me rub your feet, massage your back, rub away your sorrows with these gifted hands.

I just want you to relax, completely unwind let down your hair and release all your cares.

You're perfectly safe with me.

Relax.

~Encore Love~

Let me cater to you, serve you hand and feet.

You deserve all the best, release all your cares to me and let me serve your every command.

Relax.

Tell me what's on your mind; I'll be your therapist.

Relax.

Tell me what the day's events have been like; I am all ears for you.

Relax.

Release...

Reveal your true essence.

Confidence

When I look into your eyes I completely believe what I see.

I see an expression of love and peace in your eyes that I've longed for years to see.

I have confidence in you

That were just as the beginning of what God has for us and the half has not even been told yet.

I have confidence in you

That our brightest days are ahead and there are greater moments to be shared with you; full of laughter, full of joy.

I have confidence in you.

That you will achieve your goals, realize your dreams, and relinquish your fears.

I have confidence, so much confidence in you.

Pain

I would never obstruct your destiny.

I would never pull you away from your path.

I will always encourage you to do your best, be your best and maximize your potential.

Every now and then I get this pain.

I cry.

I weep.

I pray for better days and moments with you.

I must tell the truth and come completely clean, my heart is aching.

Pain

It seems like there's not enough hours in a day.

I know you're doing your best and we have a lot on our hands but my heart feels this pain.

Pain

When you're together with someone but feel so alone; although it's not like this every day todays just one of those days where I wish I could sleep it away.

Pain

I wish I could close my eyes and wake up to you and renew our bliss.

I wish everyday felt like the day I fell in love with you.

I'll keep praying

Yet I feel this pain.

You don't treat me bad; I just don't see you enough. I just don't hear your voice enough. I just miss the warmth of your smile.

Pain

Sometimes I feel like I am loosing myself when I really want to be with you.

I'd rather be holding you, kissing you and whispering in your ear.

Pain

I just want this aching in my heart to go away.

Today I pray, Lord I need you...

If you hear me, please help me and take this pain.

Can I Have Your Attention Please

Sitting on opposite sides of the room and everything in me wants to touch you, hold you kiss you but I won't disturb your rest.

Can I have your attention please?

Can I hold your hand, let you lie on my chest and listen to the rain?

Can I have your attention please?

Can I savor the smell of your sweet skin the way I used to?

Can I have your attention please?

Rub you down with lotion and oils and make all your aches and pains go away. How about the healing that your body needs from a long week of work.

Can I have you attention please?

Can I cuddle with you and watch our favorite T.V. show or movie.

Can I have your attention please?

Can we go for a ride in the car to the middle of nowhere just to have a quiet moment together?

Can I have your attention please?

Can you touch me like you used to?

Kiss me like you used to?

Hold my hand the way you used to?

Caress my body like you used to?

I just want your attention, your affection, your love. I feel like I am emotionally starving.

I pray that God will make everything alright and until he does, can I have your attention please?

Tonight

I need you to hold me tight

I need to feel your heat beat

I need to be held

I need to feel your body pressed against mine.

I need to feel your warmth

I need to cry with you

I need to tell you my fears

I need to pray with you

I need to make my conscious clear

I need to know what you're feeling

I need to know that our past is healing

I need you to lay your head on my chest

I need us to love like it's the last time

I need you tonight.

It's going to be alright

I know it has not been easy lately but I trust that is alright.

I know you have had to cry sometimes but believe me it's alright.

I know you felt fear gripping your chest and sometimes tears escaping your eyes, but it's alright.

I know you have to sometimes pray to make it through the day, but it's alright.

I know sometimes it gets confusing because you just can't see the way, but it's alright.

I know sometimes you have more bills than money, but it's alright.

I know sometimes you feel like your barely keeping your head above water, but it's alright.

I can feel the breaking of day coming,

I feel change near so do give up.

I can feel all your fears leaving you.

I can see us celebrating and experiencing laughter.

I can see us looking back on these days with more joy then the day we lived and experienced them.

No matter what we see or face today, hold your head up love because it's going to be alright!

I'm In Your Corner

When God gave us love he gave us a special place just for me and you. God graced us with an undying bond that will lead us and guide us to freedom.

Loneliness sometimes presents itself in the moments and times where you're nowhere near. I lock it out with all the memories we have built together looking forward to the time you come home.

Your smile brightens my day, turns the light on to my path and helps gives direction to my unsure footsteps.

I'm in your corner,

When it seems like our backs are against the wall, know that I am there with you and I am in it with you.

I'm in your corner,

Praying for you, cheering for you and expecting victories in your life daily, I'm with you.

I'm in your corner

Even when your knees buckle and you feel like you can't bear the load I am there with you holding you up.

It's me and you against the world.

I'm in your corner.

~Encore Love~

Part IV

~Encore Love~

A Beautiful Morning

Every day that I wake up to you holding you, rolling over to kiss you and smell your sweet skin my heart smiles.

It's a beautiful morning

When the sun warms my skin, from the heat I pull back the seats and stretch myself to face the duties of my day.

It's a beautiful morning

In spite of what we have had to face on yesterday, todays a new day filled with new mercies and Gods riches blessings.

It's a beautiful morning

When I feel the glow of the smile on your face, it gives me strength to fight and face another day.

It's a beautiful morning

Uttering my fist I love you to God and then my soul mate. I feel overwhelmed and grateful.

Blessed is more of the terminology to describe what I feel this day.

It's a beautiful morning

I pray over you, decree Gods riches blessings and mercies to follow your footsteps.

It's a beautiful morning

Seeing you off into your day, asking Gods angles to protect my sweet heart, I can go on and on with prayers and day dreams of you.

Ill rest my case and embrace this beautiful morning.

It's My Honor

When you have waited as long as I have waited for love you do all within your power to cherish the gift God has given you.

It's my honor to love you.

You're more than a gift to me. You're like a diamond in the ruff, pulled out the lost and found.

It's my honor to love you.

Not every man could handle you, love you, understand you and hold you. I am grateful that God saw fit to entrust me with his gem.

It's my honor to love you.

I will withhold nothing from you; I am fighting for you, pushing you into purpose and destiny.

It's my honor to love you.

There are moments I struggle with you because I feel I don't deserve you. I suffered so hard so long and unbelievable to find a love so true.

It's my honor to love you.

Ill forever hold you dear to my heart. I pray that we never part. I pray that you will always be with me.

I honor you.

I cherish you.

You're a special gift from God to me.

My duty is to be a steward over this gem.

I roll up my sleeves and assume the responsibility. It's my honor to love you.

Friction

I can feel my temperature rising and my pours begin to burst with sweat. I whisper in your ear, "I love you". My heart skips beats and like a track of our favorite love song it repeats. I feel my skin glowing. I feel a touch deeper than flesh its spiritual.

You rub my face, kiss my lips, I grab your hips and its all friction. The temperature of the room changes and sometimes there's afterglow and smoke, the smell of sweat and dew fills the room and there's no rain.

My pulse keeps racing; your trust against my body gets stronger. In the heat of the night I can't tell where my body begins and where yours begins. I can't tell where my body ends and where yours begins. Where stuck together. Were one, it's like a dream come true.

Friction...

When we make love there's an aroma in the air, there's a fire burning and sometimes it lingers. The type of fire and romance that makes you smile when you think of the night before. Or when you think of moments of our intimacy your body responds with ecstasy.

Friction...

The heat and passion of your touch stays embedded in my memory for days to come. Our laughter our cries our moans stay with me.

Friction...

The fire of desire keeps burning and I want more of you. That love stuck look in your eyes keeps me going. The appreciation of another heart beat against mines drives me wild.

Friction...

When I close my eyes I day dream of you, I see you, I smell you, I hear you and I feel you.

Friction...

Heat

You entered the room and suddenly the temperature changes. I can feel my heart racing, my skin gets moist and I am sweating bullets. You give me a glance and my world lights up, you bring the heat.

When you smile I feel the warmth of the sunshine, I feel your heat. When you touch my body I have a ripple effect of emotions. When I taste your lips I thirst for more.

Sometimes I hunger for your attention, just a moment to spend more time with you. No one in the room just me and you; just a moment to hold your hand make small talk and possibly some heat!

I want to share with you the way you make me feel and show you how much I have healed from years of brokenness and being with you has been the best days of my life. No other person has ever been able to do what you do because when you do it, you bring the heat!

This I Promise You

This I promise you

That as long as it's in my power to make a difference in your life I will.

This I promise you

That if I see you frown, I'll make you pull up a smile.

This I promise you

That you'll never go hungry, physically, mentally, spiritually, sexually and emotionally. I give you my all.

This I promise you

That every day we will make the most of it, every moment together will be enjoyable weather the days be good or bad.

This I promise you

That no other love will be compared to what we share; that we will go down in history as something great.

This I promise you

That greater is ahead of us and joy and peace will chase after us.

This I promise you

That we will never drink tears for water, if we even cry it will be out of joy or the power of the experience of letting something go for the greater.

This I promise you

That when you come home there will be peace; there will be an atmosphere that celebrates your presence.

This I promise you

That I'll always be honest always be true, always be real and I'll always love you!

Have I Told You Lately?

Have I told you lately how much I adore you?

Have I told you lately how much you mean to me?

Have I told you how much you have changed my world?

Have I told you I panic when I think of life without you?

Have I told you how much joy I receive when we come home to each other?

Have I told you life with you is like a never ending love letter or the radio playing a love song on repeat?

Have I told you how much I desire your touch, your embrace, your kiss?

Have I told you how addicted I am to you?

Have I told you that your always on my mind, my day starts and ends with thoughts of you.

~Encore Love~

Have I told you the longer were together the stronger we grow together?

Have I told you I've been delivered from fear?

Have I told you lately how much I love you?

Have I told you lately?

Have I told you?

How much I love you!

Other Books By The Author

1. Soul Cleanse Vol. 1 (Poetry)

2. Lost & Found (Poetry)

3. Life Editing Vol. 1- Taking Out The Trash

4. Called To Affluence

5. Diary Of An Ex Husband

6. The Newborn Entrepreneur

7. The Millionaire Class Vol. 1

8. Prayerology Vol. 1- The School Of Prayer

9. The Purpose Driven Prayer Life

~Encore Love~

About The Author

Dr. Michael McCain, best known as a motivational speaker, author. Yet there's more to his experience and story Dr. McCain is also a poet, entrepreneur, life coach and spiritual teacher. Michael is also an established author of several books over the last 10 years and has grown in his experience to go from print press publishing to owning his own publishing company. Michael has a wide range of experience both in business and in the non-profit religious sector. Best known as the General in the Art of Strategic Prayer and Spiritual Warfare, The Author of "Prayerology" Michael McCain is a life coach, Prophetic voice and Ambassador of Hope. Dr. Michael McCain is a 21st Century World Leader who has partnered with business moguls, politicians, church, civic and world leaders for more than 15 years to equip and empower millions to maximize their potential. As one of the leading voices of our time, he founded Dr. Michael McCain Enterprises Inc. (DMME), Maximize Publishing Inc. & Kaleo University, as well as a conglomerate of companies and business to bring practical solutions to spiritual and social ills; effecting change within our communities while transforming the course of our global destiny. His track record as a revolutionary thinker and prolific communicator, has established him as one of the most respected and sought-after youthful leaders in the world today.

Since 2010 Michael McCain has been a highly sought-after spiritual coach mentoring leaders, clergy and lay members. With his move in the publishing industry he has set himself apart not just to the church but to the world; making his life coaching experience broad enough to reach people in the pews as well as the secular marketplace. He has successfully made his mark with his books in Self Help and Empowerment as well as Spirituality and Entrepreneurship. His wisdom as insight is beyond his years and is a voice that will be remembered through generations.

~Encore Love~

www.ingramcontent.com/pod-product-compliance
Lightning Source LLC
Chambersburg PA
CBHW072209090426
42740CB00012B/2446